PATRICK H. PERRINE

Fail Fast, Recover Faster

Bouncing Back from Entrepreneurial Failure

amazonkindle

"You may encounter many defeats, but you must not be defeated. In fact, it may be necessary to encounter the defeats, so you can know who you are, what you can rise from, how you can still come out of it."

- Maya Angelou

Contents

Preface

As an entrepreneur, there's a potent cocktail of passion, vision, and risk-taking that fuels your journey. You pour your heart into a concept, a product, a service, believing deeply in its potential for success. My passion project was my third startup, DogTelligent, a venture that aimed to redefine the way we interact with our pets through technology. But despite its promise and initial success, DogTelligent was a journey that would teach me some of my most invaluable lessons in entrepreneurship.

DogTelligent fell short of its goal due to technological constraints and potential safety concerns for our furry friends. The financial loss was significant, but the hardest part was letting down the community of crowdfunding supporters who had believed in me and the vision for DogTelligent. The sting of their disappointment was sharp and deeply personal. It reached its peak when an angry supporter, left dog collar-less, sent me a death threat. Yes, a death threat – a chilling reminder that entrepreneurship can be a high-stakes game, even when the stakes are not what you expect.

But here's the thing about failure—it's an unparalleled teacher. From the ashes of DogTelligent came a wealth of wisdom about the harsh realities of entrepreneurship, about the need for both passion and pragmatism, and about resilience in the face of adversity. These lessons inspired this book, "Fail Fast, Recover Faster."

In these pages, you'll find stories of entrepreneurs who have navigated failure and emerged stronger. You'll uncover strategies for damage control, for pivoting quickly, for turning setbacks into springboards for success. I'll share with you the lessons I learned from DogTelligent and other ventures, not just about managing financial, relationship, and reputation damage, but also about dealing with the disappointment of supporters and the personal impact of failure.

Remember, every stumble presents an opportunity for growth, every failure a stepping stone towards success. I invite you to join me on this journey, to learn from our collective failures and successes, and to harness your own unique entrepreneurial journey. As we stumble smartly, recover rapidly, and race towards our next triumph, remember that your entrepreneurial journey is not just about the destination—it's also about the resilience and wisdom you gain along the way.

Happy reading!

-Patrick H. Perrine

1

So You Failed, Now What?

Failure. That monstrous apparition that's been snacking on your dreams and left you feeling like a disco dancer in a library. Indeed, an irksome, uninvited guest! But let's not scowl. Instead, throw the red carpet for this intrusive visitor. Wondering why? Because in the exhilarating roller-coaster ride of entrepreneurship, failure is as common as weak tea in a roadside diner. We've all sipped it, grimaced, and wished for a more robust brew.

Here's the silver lining. Just as the blandness of weak tea can ignite a quest for a robust chai latte, a business flop can be a slingshot, propelling us towards our most splendid success saga. So, shuffle closer, my courageous entrepreneur friend. Sure, you've slipped, you've tumbled, and now you're peering over the cliff, into the void, contemplating, "What's the game plan now?" It's high time to transform this monumental blunder into a marvelous opportunity.

It's human to feel the sting of defeat, to soak in the "woe is me" pool and engage in the 'what ifs' and 'why mes' internal dialogue. But here's a truth bomb: even the most triumphant entrepreneurs have worn your shoes, felt as blue as you do now. This isn't the apocalypse, nor the conclusion of your career – far from it! This is the dawn of a riveting, thrilling, and immensely gratifying phase in your entrepreneurial odyssey.

Take Sir Richard Branson, for instance, an emblem of entrepreneurial triumph. Are you aware of his numerous stumbles before he hit his stride? From an unsuccessful student magazine to a fizzled-out bridal company, he's taken a fair share of tumbles. Yet, there he is, soaring as the captain of the Virgin Group, a titan spanning over 400 companies. And you can bet your last dollar, he's grinning all the way to the bank!

Branson's journey tells us that the path to entrepreneurial success isn't linear. After the bridal company tanked, he could have thrown in the towel. But Branson chose to learn, pivot, and venture forth, eventually launching Virgin Records in 1972. Today, the Virgin brand encompasses music, aviation, space travel, and more. Remember this as you lick your wounds: Failure isn't a full stop, but a comma, a pause before you move on to your next exciting venture.

Now let's give a standing ovation to Elon Musk, the audacious risk-taker behind SpaceX and Tesla. This modern-day innovator has had his share of failure. SpaceX's first three launches failed, and Tesla was on the brink of bankruptcy in its early years. But Musk, armed with indefatigable spirit and unwavering belief, refused to accept defeat. Look where he stands today – at the forefront of technological innovation and a symbol of entrepreneurial resilience!

You might wonder how Musk persevered despite such setbacks. His secret lies in viewing failure not as a downfall, but as a learning opportunity, a stepping stone towards success. When rockets exploded and Tesla struggled, Musk didn't buckle.

Instead, he used these experiences to refine his strategies and build better rockets, more efficient cars. Musk's journey teaches us that when we change our perspective towards failure, we find the fuel to keep going and to innovate beyond our wildest dreams.

Much like Branson and Musk, you are an entrepreneur. A pathfinder, a daredevil, a dream-weaver. You are a valiant soul who dares to step into the unknown, traverses the road less trodden, and risks all for a vision only you can perceive. Sure, that path can get rocky, and sometimes we stumble and face-plant. But does that mean it's curtains? Nope, the drama's just cranking up.

Yes, it's heart-wrenching when our ventures disintegrate like a sandcastle caught in a rogue wave. We witness our dreams dissolve, often taking with them our nest egg, our connections, and a chunk of our sanity. But therein lies the allure of failure. It's in the wisdom it imparts, the resilience it forges, and the resolve it kindles. It's the coarse grit that polishes us into a gleaming success.

So, my tumble-weary comrade, it's time to rally. Brush off that battered ego, smooth out that troubled brow, and flash the world your most defiant grin. You may be down, but you're far from finished. With each mishap, you're inching closer to triumph. And I'm here to aid you in vaulting over that barrier and dashing towards your next colossal victory.

In this journey, you will have to dig deep. You'll have to uncover the lessons your failures offer and wield them as your weapons. You'll have to be relentless in your pursuit of success, unyielding in the face of adversity. In this new chapter of your story, remember that every failure, every stumble, is an opportunity. An opportunity to learn, to grow, to become the successful entrepreneur you were born to be.

Roll out the red carpet for your comeback story. So, you faltered? Splendid! Now, let's invert that frown and show the world the true mettle you're forged of! Let's show the world that an entrepreneur's spirit is unbreakable, that every failure brings us one step closer to our dazzling success. It's your time to rise, dear friend. Embrace your failures, embrace your journey, and become the unicorn you're destined to be.

Guided Recommendations

As you reflect upon this chapter, pause and grant yourself the grace of self-compassion. Remind yourself that every great entrepreneur has faced setbacks. Your current state is not a depiction of your ultimate destination. Right at this moment, draft a letter to yourself documenting what you have learned from this failure and how you have grown because of it. Be your cheerleader, highlighting your strengths and resilience that will steer you to your next venture. Keep this letter safe, and promise to read it whenever you find yourself in a tight spot in the future.

Secondly, identify your support system—be it friends, family, or mentors—who have stood by you. Arrange to have honest conversations with them to gain different perspectives and perhaps unearth potentials or opportunities you haven't seen yet. Their feedback can be a goldmine of inspiration and guidance as you lay the foundations for your next venture. At the same time, distance yourself from naysayers who amplify negativity; surround yourself with positivity and people who nourish your entrepreneurial spirit.

Lastly, as you take steps forward, make a habit of celebrating small victories. Setting and achieving short-term goals will not only keep you motivated but also create a trail of successes that can eventually lead to your big dream coming true. Be meticulous in your planning, and do not shy away from revisiting and tweaking your plans based on the lessons learned. Remember, resilience isn't just about bouncing back; it's about moving forward with a wiser, stronger approach, ready to seize the opportunities lying in the path ahead. Embrace the journey with an open heart, armed with the wisdom garnered from past experiences, and a firm belief in your invincible entrepreneurial spirit.

2

The Domino Effect: Understanding the Full Impact of Failure

Alright, my resilient warrior, you've had your moment of wallowing and let's be honest, who can resist a good wallow? Like a triple-scoop ice cream cone on a sunny day, it can be oh-so-satisfying. But now that we've acknowledged the beast, let's see what kind of mischief this failure monster has been up to.

You see, failure can be like that unruly houseguest who not only raids your fridge but also makes a mess of your entire house. It doesn't limit its chaos to just your professional life. Oh no, that would be too easy! It topples into your personal life, kicks around your finances, and can even take a jab at your mental health. Kind of rude, don't you think?

Let's break it down, shall we?

Personal Relationships: You know that thing about bringing work home? Sometimes it's more than just stress. The aftershocks of a business failure can ripple into your personal life, straining relationships with your partner, family, and friends. They've been on this wild ride with you, and they might feel the bumps just as hard.

Behind every successful entrepreneur, there's often a supportive network of loved ones. They celebrate your victories and help dust you off after your defeats. A business failure can cast a shadow over these relationships, as the stress and disappointment can unknowingly seep into your interactions. It's important to remember that they are your cheerleaders, not your adversaries, during these challenging times.

Finances: Ah, finances, the lifeblood of your dreams, and sometimes the first victim of your business flop. Suddenly, you're digging into your pockets, and all you're finding are crumpled receipts and loose change. Bummer, right?

Money is often considered a taboo topic, a source of discomfort. But it's crucial to face this head-on. Financial fallout from a business failure can be daunting. It can range from depleted savings to burgeoning debts. It's a difficult pill to swallow, but it's not insurmountable. With careful planning, smart strategies, and perhaps a touch of austerity, you can navigate through this storm.

Mental Health: Let's not forget about this one, your unseen but oh-so-important ally. The stress, disappointment, and anxiety from a business failure can take a toll on your mental well-being. Just remember, it's okay to not be okay. This is a big deal, and it's totally normal to feel down.

The emotional toll that failure can impose is often overlooked in the high-octane world of entrepreneurship. But ignoring it can be detrimental. Remember, it's okay to seek help, to lean on others, to take a break. This isn't a sprint but a marathon, and preserving your mental health is as important as a business strategy.

Professional Reputation: And last, but certainly not least,

there's the impact on your professional image. You might feel like you're wearing the scarlet letter 'F' for 'Failure'. But remember, every great superhero has their share of epic showdowns before they save the day.

A failed venture may feel like a blemish on your professional record. But think of it as a badge of courage instead. It's evidence of your willingness to take risks, your tenacity, and your entrepreneurial spirit. Wear it with pride, for every professional journey has its share of peaks and valleys.

Did you know that Walt Disney, the man who brought magic into our lives, was once fired for a perceived lack of imagination? Can you imagine a world without the enchantment of Disney? Exactly! Failure doesn't define us, it refines us.

Walt Disney's story serves as a reminder that the world's most successful people were often forged in the crucible of failure. Disney faced multiple business failures and even bankruptcy before finding his magic touch. Yet, his resilience and belief in his dreams gave us the iconic brand we know today.

So yes, failure is a pesky domino that can knock down multiple aspects of your life. But here's the real scoop: Just as a domino chain can create a spectacular fall, it can also trigger an impressive rise. Each one of these impacted areas, while currently a bit shaky, is also a building block for your comeback.

Consider this part of the journey as a renovation. We're stripping down the wallpaper, knocking out a few walls, and making room for something spectacular. It's a little messy now, but when it's done - wow, just wait for the reveal!

Think of it as the renovation shows you see on TV. Initially, the house looks dilapidated and hopeless. But then, with some vision, effort, and patience, it transforms into a dream home. This renovation phase is your chance to redesign, reimagine, and rebuild.

As we navigate through this winding path, remember, you're not alone in this. Just as failure visited Branson, Disney, and countless others, it has come knocking at your door too. But each one of these folks, much like the majestic phoenix, arose from the ashes, more brilliant than before. And you're up next!

Failure is not the end of your journey, but a rite of passage. It's a part of the initiation into the ranks of great entrepreneurs who have gone before you. It's a sign that you're pushing boundaries, taking risks, and daring to disrupt. So, my resilient friend, embrace this journey, for it's leading you to a destination more glorious than you ever imagined.

And remember, you're in great company. You stand shoulder to shoulder with the likes of Steve Jobs, who was once ousted from his own company, and Arianna Huffington, whose second book was rejected by 36 publishers. Each of them, like the mythical phoenix, rose from their ashes of failure, transforming their stories of defeat into tales of triumph.

Their experiences, and yours too, prove that failure, as much as it hurts, is not only survivable but can serve as a springboard to unimaginable heights. You're up next, and I can't wait to see your own phoenix rise.

Guided Recommendations

As you stand amidst the rubble of what was once your grand venture, it's essential to roll up those sleeves and get to work on yourself, first and foremost. Begin by sitting down and reflecting on how the different spheres of your life have been affected. Are personal relationships strained? Are finances feeling a bit tight? Is your mental well-being hanging by a thread? Acknowledge each aspect individually.

Firstly, let's address your personal relationships. Reach out to the people who matter to you, people who have been your pillars of support. You have perhaps been on this roller-coaster alone for too long, immersed in your efforts to stabilize your venture. Now is the time to reconnect with your loved ones, share your feelings, and listen to theirs. Create a healing circle where everyone gets to express themselves without judgment, fostering understanding and empathy.

Next, focus on your finances. It is indeed a sensitive topic, but sweeping it under the rug will only breed anxiety and stress. Arrange for a sit-down with a financial advisor if necessary, to chalk out a practical and achievable plan to steady your financial ship. Remember to include small allowances for indulgences that bring joy and relaxation. This isn't just about economic recovery but also about nurturing your spirit back to health.

For safeguarding your mental health, consider establishing a daily routine that incorporates activities that bring peace and relaxation. This could be meditation, a stroll in the park, or indulging in a hobby you love. Be patient with yourself, give yourself the time and space to heal, to rediscover the joy in little things, and to kindle the spark of hope and creativity once again. The road to recovery is as much about nurturing your mental spirit as it is about rebuilding the external aspects of your life.

Now, turning our attention to your professional reputation. Yes, it might have taken a hit, but remember that in the entrepreneurial world, resilience and the courage to stand back up are highly respected. Start rebuilding your professional network with honesty and humility. Share your story, your learnings, and your aspirations for the future. You'd be surprised at how many people would not only understand but also admire your courage and the wisdom you've gained through your experiences.

As you initiate this journey of rejuvenation, remember that every day is a new beginning, a chance to take a step, however small, towards your dream. So let's forge ahead, with the understanding that failure isn't a pit, but a ladder, a ladder that gives us a wider perspective and teaches us the true essence of success, carved from resilience, understanding, and growth.

Keep a journal during this time, documenting your progress in each area. This will not only help you keep track of your growth but also serve as a motivational tool, reminding you of how far you've come whenever you find yourself slipping into self-doubt.

Lastly, always remember, in the grand scheme of your entrepreneurial journey, this is but a small chapter. Your story is far from over; in fact, it is ready to take a more vibrant, mature, and exhilarating turn. You have the experience, the learnings, and a spirit tempered in the crucible of trials. Gear up, my resilient friend, your phoenix is ready to rise, more radiant and powerful than ever before!

3

Catching Your Breath: Acknowledging Your Emotions and Navigating the Initial Shock

Whoa, Nelly! What a ride it's been. The dust is starting to settle, and you're probably looking around at the aftermath of your entrepreneurial tumble. Kind of feels like waking up with a hangover after a wild party, doesn't it? Except instead of nursing a headache, you're nursing a battered dream and a bruised ego. And that's okay!

Feeling defeated and disoriented is an all too common aftermath of entrepreneurial failure. Just as the sun's warm rays can sometimes lead to a sunburn, the bright and adventurous journey of entrepreneurship can sometimes lead to failure. And just like nursing a sunburn, the pain can be intense, but it will pass.

Let's face it, failure, much like a surprise jellyfish sting during a delightful beach day, can pack quite the emotional punch. You might be feeling a buffet of emotions right now: shock, anger, embarrassment, anxiety, disappointment - and guess what? You have a VIP pass to feel all these emotions and more. There's no bouncer at this club saying, "Sorry, you can only bring two emotions to this party."

The whirlpool of emotions you're currently navigating is as unique as your entrepreneurial journey. Remember, these feelings, no matter how tumultuous, are valid. Let them flow, let them be, and let them guide you towards your path to healing.

Just as you wouldn't ignore a physical wound, don't brush off these emotional bruises either. Acknowledge them, feel them, let them have their moment in the spotlight. It's perfectly normal, and an important part of your healing process. Consider this the emotional ice-pack on your entrepreneurial bump.

In the realm of entrepreneurship, facing failure can be compared to an unanticipated detour on a road trip. You're forced to change course, leading you through uncharted terrains. But remember, this is not a dead-end but a path leading to new discoveries and growth opportunities.

There's no one-size-fits-all here, everyone has their own pace. Some might hop back into the saddle immediately, while others may need a bit more time to regroup. And you know what? Both are perfectly fine.

Take, for instance, the inspiring story of Thomas Edison, who famously said, "I have not failed. I've just found 10,000 ways that won't work." He faced numerous disappointments in his quest to invent the light bulb, but he acknowledged his emotions, took the time to regroup, and kept pushing forward.

Let's also draw inspiration from Ursula Burns. Rising from a humble upbringing in a New York City housing project, Burns faced an uphill battle every step of the way. Guided by a single mother who instilled in her a belief in the power of education, she pursued a degree in mechanical engineering. Her journey was one of consistent growth, as she started as an intern at Xerox and steadily climbed the corporate ladder, breaking through countless barriers. She not only became a top executive at the company but eventually its CEO, marking her place in history as the first African American woman to lead a Fortune 500 company.

And look at her now - a beacon of determination, resilience, and grace, inspiring countless individuals to break barriers and reach for the stars. You're in good company, my friend!

This chapter is all about tending to your emotional well-being, picking up the pieces, and preparing for the recovery process. It's okay to feel shaken up, it's okay to take some time, and it's absolutely okay to seek help.

In the words of the Beatles, let's take a "long and winding road" to navigate through these emotions. It's time for some good old self-care, some introspection, and perhaps a bit of ice cream or a binge-watch of your favorite show (no judgments here).

Whether it's taking a relaxing bath, going for a long walk, or journaling your thoughts, find what comforts you and let it help you heal. Self-care isn't just a trendy term; it's an essential part of your recovery journey.

At this point, you may feel like you've been through the wringer, but hold on tight. You're about to bounce back harder than a super ball thrown at full force. You're not just any entrepreneur; you're a resilient, tenacious, phoenix-like entrepreneur, ready to rise from these ashes.

Buckle up, it's time for the comeback tour, starring you! The world has seen you fall, and now it's time for it to witness your rise. Remember, the sweetest victories often follow the toughest battles. Your entrepreneurial dream may be bruised, but it's far from broken. Let's get ready for the next chapter in your extraordinary journey.

Guided Recommendations

As you find yourself at this restorative pit stop on your entrepreneurial journey, envision it as a haven where you can recharge, gathering pearls of wisdom and strength for the chapters that lay ahead. Picture yourself drawing deep, calming breaths, ready to face the exhilarating road with a spirit reborn, ready to learn, ready to forge on with determination burning brighter than before.

Take this moment to embrace a sort of self-imposed retreat. Give yourself the grace to dive deep into the ocean of your experiences, swimming through the highs and the lows, the victories, and yes, the defeats. This isn't a time for judgment but for understanding, a time to crystallize the lessons learned, both from your successes and your stumbles.

And as you reflect, open your mind to the rich tapestries of stories from others who have been in your shoes, navigating the tumultuous seas of entrepreneurship. Immerse yourself in narratives that resonate with your spirit, be it through books, interviews, or webinars. Let the stories of others wash over you, offering a fresh perspective, and perhaps a roadmap to navigate the path that lay before you.

But dear friend, this is not all about introspection and learning; it's also a time to lavish some well-deserved affection on your own spirit, nurturing it back to a vibrant state of joy and readiness. Picture yourself setting aside regular pockets of 'Me Time,' where you indulge in activities that recharge your batteries, bringing a flush of happiness and relaxation through your being.

Let's not overlook the vivacious spirit of creativity that likely spurred your entrepreneurial journey in the first place. Envision yourself rediscovering that joyous impulse, perhaps through painting, crafting, writing, or even dancing. It's about reigniting that spark, allowing yourself to explore and play without judgment or expectation, nurturing the very core of your inventive spirit.

As you continue this nurturing process, envision yourself gradually building a resilient fortress around you. It's a living, breathing entity, evolving with each new lesson, each newfound understanding, morphing and adapting as you do. This fortress stands as a testament to your journey so far, a protective shell harboring your dreams and nurturing them to fruition.

And in the stillness of your fortress, picture yourself embracing mindfulness practices that ground you, that offer a tranquil shelter from the whirlpool of emotions, giving you the clarity to see the road ahead with renewed vigor.

So here we stand, my fellow trailblazer, on the cusp of renewal, ready to forge ahead with a spirit not just revived but rejuvenated, more equipped, and vibrant with the rich tapestry of experiences woven so far. Picture yourself standing tall, not starting from scratch but from a place of deeper understanding, with a heart ready to embrace the plethora of opportunities that await.

Yes, the road ahead is undulating, perhaps fraught with challenges yet unknown. But remember, you're not the same person who started this journey. You're a warrior, resilient and enriched with experience, standing on the threshold of countless possibilities, ready to carve out a path that's uniquely yours.

So, gather your strengths, embrace your learnings, and step forward with a heart brimming with hope and a spirit dancing with possibilities. You have the wisdom of your experiences and the freshness of your revitalized spirit, ready to take on the entrepreneurial world with grace and gusto.

The adventure is far from over; in fact, it's just beginning anew. Forward, with joy, hope, and unyielding resolve, into the exciting future that awaits. Onwards and upwards, brave entrepreneur! It's time to rise, once more, with dreams untamed and spirit unbroken. Let's champion this journey together, for the best is yet to come.

4

Self-Compassion and the Art of Dusting Yourself Off

Hello there, resilient go-getter! After some well-deserved emotional TLC, it's time to roll up our sleeves, put on some energizing tunes (I'm thinking a bit of "Eye of the Tiger"), and start the process of dusting yourself off.

Imagine failure as an uninvited party guest who's overstayed their welcome, left empty snack bowls, and toppled decorations. It's an apparent mess, but look closer. The party might be over, but the experience - the music, the laughter, the dance-offs - isn't something you'd trade. Similarly, your entrepreneurial journey, though marked with failure, is an invaluable experience teeming with learning opportunities.

But guess what? We've got the best clean-up crew in town: you, powered by a heaping dose of self-compassion. Yes, you heard me right! Your number one ally in this process is a good, hearty helping of kindness towards yourself.

When the dust settles post-failure, self-criticism often looms large. It's like a spotlight shining on every misstep and miscalculation. But remember, the spotlight also illuminates the stage for a powerful performance. Here, the performance is the cultivation of self-compassion, which, like a soothing balm, helps heal the sting of failure.

It's easy to get caught up in a whirlwind of self-blame, criticism, and regret after a failure. But just as you wouldn't blame a novice cyclist for tumbling a few times, you can't blame yourself for a business failure. It's all part of the learning process.

And who knows better about this than Steve Jobs? Co-founder of Apple, the force behind revolutionary products that changed the world. He wasn't always the beacon of success we know him as today. He was, in fact, ousted from his own company, which he co-founded. But did he let this failure define him? Absolutely not.

During his time away from Apple, Jobs honed his abilities and vision by founding NeXT, a computer platform development company. His journey, punctuated by the bitterness of being pushed out from Apple and the initial lukewarm response to NeXT, taught him invaluable lessons about leadership, product development, and market demand. But instead of wallowing in regret or self-blame, he nurtured self-compassion. This crucial aspect of his recovery enabled him to make one of the most epic comebacks in the history of business, eventually leading Apple to become a global tech giant.

So, let's get that self-compassion flowing. Embrace your imperfections, forgive yourself for the mistakes, and celebrate the fact that you took a risk many dare not even contemplate. Give yourself a pat on the back for the courage, the spirit, and the tenacity you've shown.

As we embark on this clean-up journey, don't forget the

laughter. The path to recovery doesn't have to be gloomy and grey. Infuse it with light-heartedness. Find humor in your missteps, chuckle at the absurdities, and don't forget to flash that dazzling smile. After all, they say laughter is the best medicine, and who are we to argue with such age-old wisdom?

Take a page from the book of the legendary Charlie Chaplin, a master of turning trials into comedy. He said, "Failure is unimportant. It takes courage to make a fool of yourself." So go ahead, make light of the situation. It's a fantastic way to lessen the sting.

Remember, by treating yourself with kindness and humor, you're not just sweeping up the remnants of failure. You're laying the foundation for a stronger, wiser, and even more determined version of yourself. Now, doesn't that sound like someone you'd like to meet?

Get ready, dear friend. The dusting process has begun. You're not just cleaning up; you're also clearing the path for your encore. Just like an artist preparing the canvas for a masterpiece, you're setting the stage for your comeback. As you do so, the crowd - your dreams, aspirations, and potential - is buzzing with anticipation.

Guided Recommendations

Ah, here we are, ready to show some tender love and care to the one person who deserves it the most right now – yourself. Picture yourself armed with the most resilient of brooms, ready to sweep away the remnants of doubt, fear, and despair that might be lingering around, remnants from that uninvited party guest we call failure.

As you stand amidst the afterparty of your business venture, don't rush through this cleanup process. Imagine yourself doing this with a sense of respect and reverence for every experience you gained, cherishing even those mistakes because, believe it or not, they are now your most prized mentors guiding you on what not to do in the future.

As you dust off, picture yourself finding hidden treasures among the debris, treasures of wisdom, hidden insights, and yes, a rediscovered sense of humor. Oh, how vital it is to be able to laugh at oneself, to not take everything so seriously that you lose the joy and spontaneity of life.

Take a moment to reflect on the giant shoulders of the legends who have walked this path before you. Steve Jobs, a man who showed that with self-compassion, one could rise from the ashes stronger and more focused than before. Let's borrow a leaf from his book, shall we? Let's give ourselves the permission to learn, to grow, and to rise above our perceived failures, coming back even stronger and more focused.

Now, imagine yourself becoming your best friend, your most heartfelt cheerleader, encouraging yourself with kindness, understanding, and a genuine smile. Allow yourself to see the human being behind the entrepreneur, acknowledging the courage it took to venture into the uncharted waters of business.

Feel the support of your self-compassion as a warm, encouraging hand on your shoulder, guiding you, encouraging you to stand tall, to dust yourself off with grace and to prepare for the journey ahead with renewed vigor and enthusiasm. It is this self-compassion that is going to be your silent partner, supporting you every step of the way as you rebuild, reimagine, and forge ahead.

As you stand there, in the midst of the cleanup, picture yourself suddenly breaking into a dance, a dance of joy for the lessons learned, a dance of anticipation for the wonderful journey that lies ahead, a dance that celebrates the unyielding spirit within you, ready to give it another go, with more wisdom, more experience, and yes, more self-compassion.

Oh, and don't forget to laugh, to find the humor in the situation, to lighten up and not take everything so seriously. Picture yourself learning to see the lighter side of life, to smile through the cleanup process because you know that this isn't the end, but a fresh start, a new beginning.

As you stand with broom in hand, envision yourself not just as a cleaner but as a skilled artist preparing the canvas for your next masterpiece. Each stroke of the broom is a brushstroke on the canvas of your entrepreneurial journey, a journey that is far from over.

Dear resilient spirit, as we come to a close in this chapter, picture yourself standing amidst a cleaned up, revitalized space, the space of endless possibilities that your business venture can embark on. Feel the bubbling energy of anticipation, the joyous hum of dreams ready to take flight once more.

Yes, resilient go-getter, you are ready, with a heart full of self-compassion and a spirit rearing to soar. Forward we march, with broom transformed into a wand of possibilities, ready to paint the canvas of your entrepreneurial story with bold strokes of courage, wisdom, and joyful anticipation. Let's do this, with self-compassion as our guiding star, onward to a future replete with endless possibilities!

5

Deconstructing the Wreckage: Learning from Your Mistakes

Greetings, intrepid entrepreneur! With dust shaken off and spirits undimmed, it's time to delve into the richly complex labyrinth of past ventures. Welcome to the enthralling sphere of failure forensics, a journey that ingeniously transmutes the debris of past missteps into gleaming signposts of future success.

This chapter casts you in the role of an archaeologist, a detector of patterns within the rich soil of past entrepreneurial efforts. We're not here to mourn lost opportunities or assign blame. Instead, we'll methodically sift through the residue of decisions, actions, and strategies that stumbled, finding in each piece a potential gem of wisdom. In this endeavor, failure isn't a crushing dead-end; it's a stepping stone towards the sunlit uplands of future victories.

To begin, we turn our gaze to the remarkable journey of Reid Hoffman, co-founder of LinkedIn. Before shaping the world's largest professional networking platform, Hoffman navigated the rough waters of an early entrepreneurial endeavor,

SocialNet.com, an online dating and social networking site born in 1997. Despite its innovative concept, SocialNet.com failed to garner the expected traction and ultimately shuttered. Yet, Hoffman, embodying the essence of our entrepreneurial archaeologist, didn't interpret this as a crushing defeat; instead, he recognized it as a rich, fertile learning ground.

Reflecting on SocialNet's shortcomings, Hoffman understood that the venture was ahead of its time, launching into a market not quite ready for such a platform. He diligently analyzed this experience, uncovering valuable insights about market readiness, timing, and the crucial importance of aligning offerings with users' immediate needs. Armed with this new-found wisdom, Hoffman infused these lessons into LinkedIn's blueprint, effectively meeting the needs of an underserved professional networking demographic. The phenomenal success of LinkedIn and its astronomical $26.2 billion sale to Microsoft stand as glowing testimonials to Hoffman's resilience, sagacity, and adeptness at learning from past failure.

Yet, Hoffman is but one of the many stars in our entrepreneurial firmament. Lighting our path alongside him is the inspirational Arlan Hamilton, founder of Backstage Capital. Hamilton's journey into the realm of venture capitalism was far from smooth. She braved numerous rejections, weathered the brutal storm of homelessness, and stared down the systemic biases prevalent in her industry while attempting to establish Backstage Capital. For many, such adversities would spell the end of the dream. Not for Hamilton.

Hamilton, with her indomitable spirit, took each rejection as a challenge, each setback as an opportunity to grow stronger. She delved deep into the biases that dominated her industry, using her insights to fuel her desire to level the playing field for marginalized entrepreneurs. Every 'no' she heard, every door that closed in her face, was a lesson - lessons about grit, tenacity, the fight against prejudice, and the unwavering faith in her vision.

Hamilton's resilience bore fruit. Today, Backstage Capital has invested in over 150 startups helmed by underrepresented entrepreneurs. Her journey is a powerful testament to the transformative power of learning from setbacks and using those insights as a springboard to unprecedented heights of success.

Remember, your entrepreneurial journey doesn't terminate at the borders of a failed venture. It merely heralds a new phase, a transformative journey where you dissect past experiences, distilling invaluable lessons. This journey isn't about self-flagellation but about treasure hunting, with each lesson discovered guiding you toward the next peak of success.

So, arm yourself with an open mind, an analytical eye, and an unwavering zeal for learning. This voyage into your past ventures is about transmuting setbacks into setups for victories yet to come. The wisdom gleaned from your past missteps forms the secret recipe of your future triumphs.

Brace yourself for the revelations to come, and dive headfirst into this quest of exploration and self-discovery. The road to success is paved with lessons extracted from the past. Immerse yourself in this transformative process of morphing past mistakes into future victories. The journey continues, dear courageous entrepreneur. Every stumble, every detour, every misstep you've faced is but a stepping-stone in the path to your castle of success.

Guided Recommendations

Welcome, insightful explorer, to the reflection chamber of your entrepreneurial journey. As we prepare to delve deeper, navigating the intricate labyrinth of your experiences, let us gear ourselves with the wisdom of learning from our missteps, armed with the mighty shield of self-compassion and the sword of insight to cut through the tangles of past decisions.

Imagine yourself as a seasoned archaeologist, equipped with a meticulous eye and a gentle brush, ready to uncover the hidden gems buried in the soils of your past experiences. As you embark on this excavation, remember to treat each find, each fragment of past endeavors, not as a relic of failure, but as a beacon of knowledge, guiding your way forward.

As you carefully sift through your entrepreneurial soil, take moments to analyze each fragment you come across. Perhaps you find a shard from a product that didn't launch successfully — can you identify the mismatch in market demands that led to its downfall? Or maybe you stumble upon remnants of a marketing strategy that didn't resonate; what can you discern about the preferences and needs of your audience from this?

To bring a more structured approach to your excavation, create a map of your entrepreneurial landscape, marking the spots where you faced setbacks. Then, one by one, visit each site with a compassionate and analytical mindset, unraveling the layers of experiences and unveiling the lessons hidden therein.

While you journey, draw inspiration from Reid Hoffman, who turned the pages of an unsuccessful chapter to pen a success story with the lessons he gleaned. Envision yourself embracing the same mindset, viewing your experiences not as failures but as learning grounds, fertile with insights and ripe with opportunities for growth.

Remember to keep the spirit of resilience alive, akin to the unyielding spirit exhibited by Arlan Hamilton. As you dissect past endeavors, visualize yourself embracing each lesson with the same vigor, the same determination to rise against all odds, and craft a path that echoes with success, learning, and empowerment.

Allow yourself to sit with each experience, understanding that this journey of analysis and reflection isn't a sprint but a marathon, a careful procession through the annals of your business history, absorbing the nuances, the finer details that went unnoticed in the hurly-burly of entrepreneurial pursuits.

Document your discoveries meticulously, creating a journal of insights that narrate the enriched story of your entrepreneurial journey, illustrating not just the hurdles but the silver linings, the learning points, and the strengths acquired through each stage.

And as you step out of this archaeological expedition, feel a newfound sense of strength and enlightenment enveloping you. You are no longer walking empty-handed but carrying a treasure trove of knowledge, a rich tapestry woven with golden threads of lessons gleaned from past experiences, ready to guide your next steps in the entrepreneurial dance.

Dear intrepid entrepreneur, as you close this chapter, take a deep, revitalizing breath. You have not just journeyed through pages of a book but traversed the rich landscapes of your entrepreneurial journey, armed with newfound wisdom and a heart brimming with courage, ready to carve a path that is informed, resilient, and destined for success.

As you forge ahead, keep this treasure trove close to your heart, a living testament to your resilience, a repository of valuable insights ready to illuminate your path as you step forward into a future beaming with opportunities, ready to write your success story with golden letters of wisdom gleaned from your past. Let's forge ahead, with the insights of the past lighting our path to a triumphant future.

6

Climbing Out of the Financial Hole: The Entrepreneur's Guide to Fiscal Fitness

Greetings, financial explorers! Ready to embark on a thrilling ascent towards financial recovery? It's time to trade our magnifying glasses for climbing gear, setting our sights on the towering fiscal Kilimanjaro. The climb might seem arduous, but armed with the right tools, it's a journey we're more than prepared to conquer!

Let's frame our financial recovery as meticulously assembling a 3D jigsaw puzzle. We start from the base, each piece methodically joining the others, slowly shaping our financial edifice into something truly inspiring. This journey isn't a sprint; it's a marathon. We're not in pursuit of fleeting fortunes or riding the volatile waves of risky investments. Instead, we're gradually constructing a durable financial structure capable of weathering economic storms.

As we embark on our journey, the first base camp is titled 'Budgeting and Cutting Back'. It's here we get up close and personal with our expenses. We'll scrutinize them, dissect them, and even confront them. The better acquainted we are with our cash flow, the easier it becomes to identify potential areas to trim expenditure. Remember, this process isn't about financial starvation; it's about making smart, strategic monetary decisions that lay a firm foundation for our climb.

Our next climb is towards the 'Debt Management' plateau. This phrase might sound like a chilling thriller, but it's more akin to an 'Ocean's Eleven' style strategic plot. Navigating debt can be intimidating, but with a well-thought-out plan and patience, it's a beast we can tame. We'll analyze our debts, prioritize them, and then tackle them one at a time. Every cent paid back propels us further on our ascent.

Finally, we reach the peak: 'Rebuilding and Growth'. Having pruned our expenses and harnessed our debts, we're now ready to stimulate growth. This stage is the shining moment for your entrepreneurial prowess. Here, we'll explore various avenues to bolster our income – a side gig, a new venture, or wise investments. As our fiscal altitude increases, the mantra for survival remains constant: save, invest, and budget judiciously.

Guiding us on this venture are two trailblazers who have navigated their fair share of financial valleys and peaks: Andrew Carnegie and Martha Stewart.

Andrew Carnegie, the son of a poor Scottish weaver, immigrated to the United States as a child. He began his journey to prosperity as a bobbin boy in a cotton factory, earning a meager $1.20 a week. Carnegie embodied the American dream, ascending from his humble origins to become one of the wealthiest individuals in history. His story underpins the power of prudent money management and intelligent investments.

A devotee of the 'Gospel of Wealth,' Carnegie believed in the compounding effect of reinvesting profits into his businesses to fuel growth, a lesson critical for our financial rebuilding phase. He once said, "The man who dies rich, dies disgraced." Carnegie spent the last two decades of his life giving away 90% of his wealth, an inspiring testament to his belief in philanthropy, a possible adjunct to our financial ascent.

Next, we turn to Martha Stewart, the reigning queen of lifestyle branding. In 2004, Stewart found herself at the center of a scandal that led to a five-month prison sentence for insider trading. For many, this would have signaled the end of their professional trajectory. But not for Stewart.

Stewart's triumphant comeback is a masterclass in debt management and reputation recovery, crucial aspects of our financial journey. Upon her release, she launched a plethora of new ventures, including TV shows and merchandise lines, reinstating her brand and herself as a household name. Her tenacity teaches us the importance of resilience in the face of adversity, a critical lesson when climbing our fiscal Kilimanjaro.

Part of her brand resurgence involved embracing unlikely partnerships, showcasing her versatility and savvy business acumen. Perhaps most notably is her unexpected yet remarkably successful partnership with rapper and entrepreneur, Snoop Dogg. This dynamic duo has not only cooked up tantalizing dishes on their Emmy-nominated television show but also explored innovative business ventures together, even in the budding cannabis industry where Stewart has developed a line of CBD wellness products. This collaboration, which perfectly juxtaposes the homely brand of Martha with the cool, hip-hop aura of Snoop Dogg, is a testament to the magic that can happen when diversity meets synergy. They teach us that with a pinch of creativity and a dash of courage, we can blend different elements, even those that seemingly clash, to create a brand that is not just unique, but phenomenally successful. It's a lesson in leveraging one's brand, understanding the pulse of the market, and not being afraid to venture into uncharted territories. Let this friendship inspire you to think outside the box, foster unexpected alliances, and venture boldly into innovative spheres as you build your financial fortress.

Climbing out of a financial pit can be an intimidating endeavor. However, as history shows, the most daunting of mountains have been conquered by those armed with determination, perseverance, and a plan. Equipped with the right tools, roadmap, and spirit, your climb to financial recovery is not just achievable; it's inevitable.

So, tighten those climbing harnesses, fellow fiscal climbers. The summit of financial recovery beckons, and with Carnegie and Stewart as our guides, we have the inspirations to make the ascent. We're not just climbing a mountain; we're building a financial future. Let the ascent begin!

Guided Recommendations

Dear fellow mountaineer on the path of financial recovery, as we stand at the culmination of this chapter, let's take a moment to reflect and strategize for the journey ahead. We have acquainted ourselves with the essential steps to fiscal recovery, imbibing valuable insights from the stalwarts in the business world, Andrew Carnegie and Martha Stewart.

Now, it is time to steer your own course, using the knowledge acquired as your compass. As you prepare to embark on this thrilling ascent towards financial robustness, remember that the journey is equally as important as the destination. Equip yourself with the tool of meticulous budgeting, ready to sculpt a financial edifice that is both durable and resilient.

Here's how you can guide yourself through the undulating journey of financial rejuvenation:

As you traverse the undulating path toward financial rejuvenation, you may find comfort and guidance in adopting a series of personal strategies rooted in attentiveness and adaptability.

Begin your journey with a focus on budgeting and cutting back, where it is crucial to take a detailed inventory of all your expenses. Split them into two categories: essential and non-essential. It will serve as a roadmap, helping you distinguish between needs and wants, fostering a culture of informed and thoughtful decisions around expenditure. Ask yourself — are there more cost-effective alternatives to your current spending habits?

Next, venture into the realm of debt management. Embark on this phase with a meticulous listing of all your debts, ranking them based on their interest rates and outstanding amounts. Developing a strategy for repayment becomes your cornerstone here. Consider concentrating your efforts on clearing high-interest debts first, lightening the financial burden incrementally and fostering a future free of the shackles of unmanaged debt.

As you emerge from the shadows of debt, step into the light of rebuilding and growth. Allow yourself to delve deep into the ocean of investment avenues, understanding their intricacies and leveraging them for your benefit. Reflect on the teachings of our guides, Carnegie and Stewart, drawing inspiration and possibly, adopting Carnegie's principles of reinvesting profits and embracing philanthropy. Ask yourself what lessons of resilience and brand management you can assimilate from

Stewart's comeback story?

The journey doesn't end here, for the path to financial rejuvenation is paved with continuous learning. Adopt a mindset of perpetual education, constantly broadening your understanding of financial matters to remain adept at managing your fiscal health effectively. Along this path, don't hesitate to seek mentorship or advice from individuals who have successfully navigated financial turmoil, for wisdom shared is wisdom amplified.

Lastly, don't overlook the power of creative alliances. Let your imagination wander, perhaps drawing inspiration from the unlikely yet successful partnership of Martha Stewart and Snoop Dogg. Consider how collaborative efforts can enhance your brand value and open up fresh avenues for growth. Keep a vigilant eye on market trends, ready to showcase flexibility and creativity in your business approach, adapting, and evolving to the pulses and rhythms of the market.

Through a tapestry woven with threads of informed decisions, strategic planning, continuous learning, and creative alliances, guide yourself tenderly, yet firmly, on a path of financial rejuvenation, rich with opportunities and growth.

As you close this chapter, envision yourself embarking on a transformative journey, where every step forward, however small, brings you closer to the pinnacle of financial stability and growth.

Keep the stories of Carnegie and Stewart close to your heart, drawing inspiration from their perseverance, adaptability, and genius as you carve out your path of financial resurgence. Remember, every financial giant started with a single step of courage and a determination to climb higher against all odds.

Embrace the climb, dear entrepreneur. With each stride, you

are not just climbing out of the financial hole; you are paving the pathway to a future of economic security and unparalleled success. Let's forge onward, climbing steadily, one strategic step at a time, towards the summit of financial stability and growth. Onward, to a future forged with financial wisdom and resilience! Let the ascent continue, steadfast and unstoppable!

7

The Relationship Aftermath: Healing and Strengthening Bonds

Greetings, budding relationship therapists! After our fiscal climb, it's time to turn our attention to the emotional landscape of your life. More specifically, we're going to focus on relationships and their essential role in your entrepreneurial recovery journey. Intrigued? You should be!

Running a business can feel a lot like juggling flaming swords while riding a unicycle. When things don't go as planned, those around you can bear the brunt of the heat. But fear not! We're about to replace those flaming swords with a soothing balm, and transform that unicycle into a tandem bicycle of trust and understanding.

Start by recognizing the strain your entrepreneurial journey may have exerted on your relationships. Whether it's a spouse, a friend, a business partner, or an investor, it's crucial to acknowledge the impact and extend a sincere, heartfelt apology where necessary. There's power in owning your mistakes and expressing regret, it sets the stage for healing.

Next, we delve into Understanding and Communication. It's a universal truth that many people don't fully grasp the life of an entrepreneur: the high stakes, the potential rewards, the late nights, and early mornings. It's our duty to help them see our world through our lens. Open up lines of communication, share your experiences, and most importantly, listen to their perspectives. As the old adage goes, "We have two ears and one mouth so that we can listen twice as much as we speak."

Then, we pedal towards Rebuilding Trust. This isn't an overnight journey; it requires consistent effort, authenticity, and patience. Transparency is key: share your progress, let them witness you applying the lessons you've learned. Step by step, you'll see the restoration of faith that might have been shaken.

Finally, we reach Strengthening Bonds. This is where the magic happens. Celebrate the wins, acknowledge the losses, and remind them (and yourself) of the immense value they bring to your life. There's no better way to reinforce a relationship than by expressing genuine appreciation and love.

Let's consider the journey of Travis Kalanick, the co-founder and former CEO of Uber. In 2017, amid a whirlwind of controversies and an internal revolt, Kalanick was asked to step down from his leadership role. The fallout affected not only his professional reputation but also significantly strained his relationships with board members, employees, and the larger startup community.

Kalanick embarked on a journey to mend these strained relationships. He took time for introspection, recognizing his mistakes, understanding his shortcomings, and issued sincere apologies for his behavior. He opened up lines of communication, sought to rebuild trust by demonstrating his commitment to change, and patiently weathered the criticism and skepticism.

Gradually, his efforts bore fruit. Relationships began to heal, and by 2018, he managed to secure funding for his next venture, CloudKitchens. Not all accepted his apologies or trusted his transformation, but those who did became part of his new journey, demonstrating the power of reconciliation and relationship-building.

Another entrepreneur who navigated a similar path is Brian Chesky, co-founder and CEO of Airbnb. During the Covid-19 pandemic, Airbnb's revenue plummeted as global travel came to a grinding halt. Chesky had to make the difficult decision to lay off nearly 25% of Airbnb's staff, a move that strained his relationships with many employees.

Chesky handled this difficult situation with empathy and transparency. In a public letter addressing the layoffs, he acknowledged the pain caused, explained the rationale behind the decision, and extended his sincere apologies to those affected. Additionally, Airbnb provided generous severance packages and launched a public talent directory to help laid-off employees find new jobs. Chesky's handling of this crisis exemplified a balance between difficult entrepreneurial decisions and maintaining relationship integrity.

Through the stories of Travis Kalanick and Brian Chesky, we see the power of acknowledging mistakes, maintaining transparency, and taking tangible steps towards rebuilding trust. They show us that relationships, even when strained, can be healed and strengthened through time, effort, and sincerity.

So, gear up to heal, communicate, rebuild, and strengthen. Your relationships, like you, are resilient. They have the capacity to bounce back stronger from adversity. Together, you're ready to embark on the next chapter of your entrepreneurial journey!

Guided Recommendations

As you find yourself on the cusp of a journey to mend and nurture your relationships, it is pivotal to walk this path with an open heart, genuine readiness for growth, and a spirit brimming with humility and understanding.

Begin with the imperative step of offering a heartfelt apology. This initial step is vital; it necessitates a detailed reflection to pinpoint the relationships that have been shadowed during your entrepreneurial endeavor. Approach this phase with a profound sense of understanding and preparedness to not only express your feelings but also to actively embrace the perspectives of others. Craft a setting that is calm and conducive for such important discussions where mutual respect is the cornerstone. It is not just about articulating regret but fostering a landscape for reciprocal understanding and empathy.

Following the heartfelt apologies, the focus shifts to resurrecting open lines of communication. Encourage a two-way dialogue where you are as engaged in conveying your viewpoint as in listening actively to others. It is about nurturing a relationship where mutual respect and understanding are held paramount. Show that you are genuinely listening, perhaps through affirmative nods or echoing what you've heard to show understanding — actions that demonstrate a willingness to forge a deeper connection.

As the threads of communication begin to weave again, the critical phase of rebuilding trust through transparency comes into play. At this juncture, the consistency of your actions paired with genuine efforts gradually builds the trust that may have eroded over time. Venture into this phase with a readiness to share not just your victories but also the lessons learned from failures, creating a space of vulnerability that fosters a deeper bond.

Transitioning to the stage of reinforced bonding, it is essential to take conscious strides to cherish and acknowledge shared victories and be a pillar of support during hardships. Make an effort to celebrate the achievements of your loved ones, fostering a symbiotic growth where mutual respect and admiration are nourished through positive affirmations and gestures of thankfulness.

As this chapter comes to a close, it invites you to personalize the guidance provided into a 'Relationship Revitalization Plan.' Envision it as a tailored roadmap, encompassing actionable strategies aligning with each phase discussed in this journey to rebuild relationships that have been strained. Be it through heartfelt letters expressing apologies, regular catch-up sessions to build a rhythm of open communication, or being transparent about your journey — each step should be finely attuned to the unique dynamics of each relationship.

Embark on this nurturing path with an attentive heart, ready to foster relationships that not only stand the test of time but emerge stronger and more harmonious than before. Let this guide lead you in nurturing relationships that radiate warmth, mutual respect, and a harmonious growth, where connections are not just revived but rejuvenated to blossom with renewed vigor and affection. It is time to commence this voyage of healing and rejuvenated connections; a journey steeped in empathy, understanding, and renewed bonds of affection.

8

The Healing Process: Self-Care and Personal Growth

Bonjour, intrepid self-care explorers! Having climbed financial mountains and navigated the stormy seas of relationships, it's time to turn our compass inward. We're setting sail towards the lush, often overlooked landscape of self-care and personal growth. Remember, a healthy entrepreneur is a successful entrepreneur!

Imagine yourself as a garden. The soil symbolizes your mind, the water embodies your emotional wellbeing, and the sunlight signifies your physical health. Too much or too little of any can disrupt your entrepreneurial ecosystem. But with the right care and balanced attention, you can bloom into an entrepreneurial powerhouse!

We begin our journey by examining your soil - Mental Wellbeing. It's the cornerstone of your recovery journey and the foundation of your entrepreneurial growth. This involves acknowledging and managing stress, seeking professional help if necessary, and harnessing the power of mindfulness and meditation. The mind, after all, is the control center of our lives, and maintaining its health and balance is paramount.

Next, we ensure the garden is properly hydrated. Emotional Wellbeing, though often overshadowed in the cacophony of entrepreneurial life, is as vital as sunlight. Grant yourself permission to feel, to vent, to laugh, to cry. Embrace your emotions, they're not your enemies but allies on this journey. Emotional balance fosters resilience, equipping you to handle the ups and downs of entrepreneurship with grace.

Now, let's bask in the sunshine! Physical Wellbeing isn't just about rigorous gym routines or guzzling kale smoothies. It's about listening to your body, allowing it the rest it requires, the nutrition it craves, and the movement it relishes. Healthy dietary habits, regular exercise, and sufficient rest form the triad of physical wellbeing, promoting overall health and boosting productivity.

Lastly, don't forget to Grow. Personal development, acquiring new skills, and seeing your mistakes as stepping stones towards growth - these elements are the fertilizers that ensure your entrepreneurial garden flourishes. Embrace lifelong learning, for every new skill, every piece of knowledge gained, fortifies your entrepreneurial prowess.

To illustrate these concepts, let's delve into the story of Arianna Huffington again. In 2007, after a collapse from burnout and exhaustion, Huffington made a pivotal decision to prioritize her wellbeing above all else. This revelation led her to found Thrive Global, a company focused on ending the burnout epidemic by providing science-based strategies for wellbeing and performance.

Huffington's journey underscores the crucial role of self-care in not just recovery, but also sustained entrepreneurial success. She reshaped her life, making space for mindfulness practices, quality sleep, and regular digital detoxes. Her transformation illuminated the connection between personal wellbeing and professional productivity, leading her to author books on the subject and passionately advocate for a balanced lifestyle in the corporate world.

In tandem with Huffington's journey, let's explore the narrative of Jack Dorsey, the co-founder of Twitter and Square. Known for his extraordinary work ethic, Dorsey also faced challenges balancing his responsibilities with his personal health. With time, he realized the importance of a balanced lifestyle, incorporating regular exercise, meditation, and a consistent sleep schedule into his routine.

Dorsey also mastered the art of time management, implementing 'theme days' to focus his attention and reduce task-switching inefficiencies. This focus on personal growth and self-care, coupled with time management, allows him to successfully steer two major companies while maintaining his wellbeing. Dorsey's journey provides valuable lessons in balance, demonstrating that taking care of oneself can coexist with entrepreneurial ambition.

The real-life experiences of Arianna Huffington and Jack Dorsey elucidate that self-care and personal growth aren't just peripherals to the entrepreneurial journey, but lie at its very heart. Their stories illustrate the essential truth that investing in your mental, emotional, and physical wellbeing isn't a luxury, but a prerequisite for sustainable success.

So, are you ready to embark on this enlightening journey of self-care and growth? Let's cultivate a healthy, thriving entrepreneurial garden together. After all, it's the garden's vitality that determines the richness of its harvest.

Guided Recommendations

As you stand on the threshold of nurturing your garden of self-care and personal growth, consider the lessons we can glean from the experiences of entrepreneurs like Arianna Huffington and Jack Dorsey, whose journeys towards wellbeing became pivotal in their entrepreneurial paths. Let us carefully glean actionable strategies, grounded in the central takeaways of this chapter, to foster your own garden of personal growth and self-care.

Think of the ways you can nurture the 'soil' of your mental wellbeing. Following in the footsteps of Arianna Huffington, who rediscovered the transformative power of mindfulness, you might establish a daily practice of meditation or mindful breathing. These simple yet profound steps can become your anchor, grounding you in tranquility amidst the bustling entrepreneur life.

As you traverse deeper, you come to the heart of emotional well-being. Just as Jack Dorsey learned to tune into his emotional landscape, it might be fruitful for you to cultivate a safe space to express your emotions freely — be it a personal journal or a trusted circle of friends and family. Embrace the full spectrum of your feelings, allowing yourself the grace to experience joy and sorrow in equal measure.

Next, we step into the realm of physical well-being. Inspired by Dorsey's lifestyle transformation, perhaps you can forge a personal routine that marries both movement and rest harmoniously. It doesn't have to be a rigid gym routine; even a leisurely walk in the park or a dance class could be avenues to foster physical health. Listen to your body's unique rhythms, offering it the nourishment and rest it seeks to bloom vibrantly in your entrepreneurial garden.

Lastly, we venture into the nurturing embrace of personal growth. Picture yourself adopting a learner's mindset, open and receptive to the treasures hidden in every experience. Embrace the spirit of lifelong learning, perhaps through enrolling in a workshop or setting aside time daily for reading and self-reflection. Remember, every step in personal growth, be it small or significant, is a fertile ground fostering your entrepreneurial bloom.

As we gently guide you on this path, we encourage you to weave these actionable strategies into the rich tapestry of your daily life. The journey of self-care and personal growth is deeply personal and uniquely yours, yet grounded in universal experiences of well-being. As you foster your garden, envisage the harvest of rich personal fulfillment and sustained entrepreneurial success that is not just possible but awaiting you.

Let us walk this path together, nurturing your garden with love, patience, and the shared wisdom of those who have walked before us, sowing the seeds for a harvest rich in personal fulfillment and entrepreneurial success.

9

The Phoenix Phase: Building Resilience and Bouncing Back

Greetings, future phoenixes! Together, we've charted territories ranging from the handling of failure, the mending of relationships, to the indispensable art of self-care. Now, we approach the juncture where we master the art of resurrection, emerging from the ashes stronger, bolder, and more resilient. Welcome to the Phoenix Phase - the craft of bouncing back!

Entrepreneurs, by their very nature, are stubborn optimists. We see silver linings even in the densest of clouds, believe in the magic of second chances, and embrace the allure of 'what could be.' As we embark on this chapter, I invite you to harness your innate optimism, kindle your courage, and learn the art of rising from the ashes like the majestic phoenix.

As I ventured into this very Phoenix Phase myself after the closure of DogTelligent, there were moments laden with self-doubt, moments where I feared I wouldn't rise again. It was during this trying time that I chose to engrave a vivid reminder of resilience on myself — a tattoo of a majestic and colorful

Phoenix, stretching from my chest, across my shoulder and back, spiraling down into a half sleeve on my arm. Every morning, as I stand before the mirror, this Phoenix greets me, its vibrant hues serving as a stalwart guard against defeatism, a symbol of rebirth and relentless spirit inked into my very skin. It whispers to me, an immutable reminder that like the mythical bird, I possess the power to rise from the ashes, to rebuild and to emerge more radiant and spectacular than before. It's more than just art; it's a piece of unyielding strength, a colorful tapestry of resilience woven from failures, learnings, and the undying belief in the potential of what could be once again. As we navigate through this chapter, I invite you to find your phoenix, your undying flame within, and to carry it with you as you forge your path through the trials and tribulations of entrepreneurship.

Our Phoenix Phase ignition begins with Acceptance. This stage involves confronting your failure, acknowledging it, and rather than viewing it as a boulder blocking your path, seeing it as a stepping stone towards your next venture. Remember, denial isn't a river in Egypt, and it certainly isn't a viable strategy for entrepreneurs.

Following acceptance, we journey into the realm of Self-Efficacy. This stage revolves around fostering the belief in your capacity to bounce back. It's akin to learning to ride a bike - remember the countless falls? And yet, you got back up each time, didn't you? Apply the same relentless determination to your entrepreneurial journey, albeit with potentially a few more zeros at stake!

Once the seeds of self-efficacy are sown, we advance to Resilience Building. This crucial phase involves finding strategies to adapt to failure, extracting valuable lessons from it, and developing mental and emotional fortitude. It's time to don the armor of resilience, constructed from the very failures you've encountered.

The final stage of our phoenix journey is the Action Phase. This is the moment you've been preparing for, where you apply all the insights gleaned, establish fresh goals, and embark on your next venture. In essence, this is where you rise, like the proverbial phoenix, stronger and more resolute than ever.

To illuminate these phases, let's delve into the journey of Howard Schultz, the visionary behind Starbucks. Schultz's path to establishing Starbucks as a global brand was strewn with rejections and failures. Yet, his tale is not one of defeat, but of indefatigable resilience.

Starting from humble beginnings as a bartender, Schultz held onto his dream of bringing Italian coffeehouse culture to America. When he first proposed the idea to the original owners of Starbucks, it was rejected. Unfazed, Schultz ventured to open his own coffeehouse, Il Giornale. Eventually, he acquired Starbucks and transformed it into the global phenomenon we know today. Schultz's journey underscores the power of resilience and the magic of bouncing back, demonstrating how initial setbacks can morph into unparalleled success.

Pivoting to another entrepreneurial titan, let's explore the story of Jack Ma, the founder of Alibaba. Ma's story is one of relentless perseverance despite repeated rejections and failures. He was turned down by Harvard ten times, rejected from multiple jobs, including KFC, and his first two ventures failed. However, Ma held onto his vision of creating an internet company for China.

When he founded Alibaba in his apartment in 1999, it was met with skepticism and faced stiff competition from established firms. Yet, Ma's indomitable spirit and unwavering belief in his venture led him to turn Alibaba into one of the world's largest e-commerce platforms. His story serves as a testament to the power of resilience and the ability to rise from the ashes of failure.

In the grand scheme of entrepreneurship, failure is not the end of the road but a detour leading to unexplored territories. The stories of Howard Schultz and Jack Ma provide invaluable lessons in resilience, demonstrating how the ashes of failure can serve as the fertile ground for new, thriving ventures.

So, are we ready to roll up our sleeves and embrace our Phoenix Phase? Remember, the essence of entrepreneurship isn't just about avoiding falls but in learning how to rise each time we stumble. Let's rise, stronger and more resolved, as the phoenix does from its ashes.

Guided Recommendations

In this pivotal chapter where we embrace the Phoenix Phase, the journey of bouncing back with renewed strength and determination takes center stage. Let us hold hands as we journey together, nurturing the resilient spirit that lives within all entrepreneurs, as we draw both inspiration and actionable strategies from the unyielding journeys of Howard Schultz and Jack Ma.

In the initial stages of this Phoenix Phase, the first step beckons: acceptance. As we stand here, perhaps we can take a moment to candidly acknowledge the hurdles we have encountered. Let us tenderly embrace our failures, not with resentment but with understanding and gratitude for the lessons they brought us. Consider journaling your feelings and reflections as a healing strategy, allowing you to move forward with a heart lightened of burdens.

Embarking further into the phase of self-efficacy, it is here where we foster an unwavering belief in our abilities to rise again. Drawing from Schultz's relentless spirit and vision, we too can harbor dreams big enough to overcome rejections. It may be beneficial to surround ourselves with mentors and peers who nurture our self-belief, forming a support system that echoes with affirmations of our strength and potential.

As we steer into the stage of resilience-building, we might take a page from Jack Ma's story, cultivating a spirit indomitable in the face of rejections. Can we, perhaps, develop a ritual of resilience, where we list down the lessons learned from each setback, converting them into stepping stones for our future ventures? Remember, each lesson is a feather in your phoenix's wing, adding to the strength that propels you to soar higher.

Then, with wings spread wide, we step into the action phase, where dreams take flight grounded in lessons learned and a spirit renewed. Here, we could envisage setting clear and attainable goals, yet with the daring to reach for the stars. Reflect on the strategies Schultz and Ma employed, and let your mind brew innovative plans, visualizing the path that leads to your dream with clarity and conviction.

As we stand on the brink of renewal, it is imperative to remember that your phoenix is unique, adorned with feathers of resilience, each telling a story of courage, perseverance, and tenacity. You might find it nurturing to personalize your phoenix journey, perhaps through art or poetry, creating a symbol that resonates with your spirit, a tangible reminder of the fiery spirit that resides within.

As we walk this path of the Phoenix Phase, embrace the fiery spirit with kindness, nourishing it with self-belief and tenacity. The nurturing guidance offered in this chapter beckons you to forge your unique path of resilience, with the encouraging whispers of your inner phoenix, guiding you to rise from the ashes, more radiant and magnificent than ever before. Together, let's craft our phoenix narratives, prepared to rise, renewed and resplendent, from the ashes of our experiences, ready to soar into the skies of boundless possibilities.

10

The Phoenix Rises: Unveiling Your New Venture

Hail, audacious phoenixes! Our shared journey has been long and winding, coursing through acceptance, resilience, and invaluable lessons strewn along the path. Now, the time has dawned for your rebirth, for spreading those fiery wings wide to embrace the sky with renewed vigor and boundless potential. Poised on the precipice of unveiling your new venture, we join forces to ignite the flames of your rise to grandeur. Make no mistake, this journey promises to be nothing short of legendary.

Embarking on a new venture after experiencing failure is akin to navigating uncharted waters under a starlit sky. It's a fusion of raw thrill and apprehension, propelling you towards the much-desired prize of accomplishment. With hearts ablaze and spirits soaring, are you prepared to dive headfirst into this exhilarating new beginning?

Our initial foray is into the world of planning - the Blueprint Phase. Here, we glean insights from past missteps, survey the landscape for new opportunities, and consciously craft a resilient business plan. In the grand scheme of entrepreneurship, a well-fortified defense often fosters the strongest offense. Your business plan is your fortress, shielding you against the turbulent tides of the market's unpredictability.

As we forge ahead, we transition into the vital phase of Team Building. In this stage, synergy and collaboration take precedence as you handpick individuals ready to share your vision and ride the waves of uncertainty with you. Seek out comrades with a fervor equal to yours, ready to unite under the phoenix banner and foster a harmonious, empowered workplace where every member contributes their distinctive strengths.

Next, we navigate the intricate labyrinth of Financing and Bootstrapping. Attracting the right investors and safeguarding against looming financial challenges is a pivotal yet challenging endeavor on this transformative journey. Wise resource management is your ally in the phoenix's ascent, guiding you in building a formidable and sustainable financial foundation.

Our path leads us to the vibrant world of Launching and Marketing, where you will proudly showcase your venture to the world. It is here that you weave a compelling narrative of resurgence, using savvy marketing strategies to construct a robust foundation for your enterprise, ready to reach towering heights of success.

To vividly illustrate these phases, let's draw from the powerful narratives of Sophia Amoruso and Sara Blakely. Amoruso rebounded from the downfall of Nasty Gal, steering her energies into the creation of Girlboss Media, a beacon for women in business. Sara Blakely metamorphosed rejection and limited resources into Spanx, a brand now synonymous with innovation and empowerment. Their journeys, steeped in tenacity and fresh perspectives, are vibrant testaments to the heights reachable through determination and a readiness to adapt.

Take heart from their paths as we step into our next segment, ready to carve your phoenix narrative with the wisdom accrued from previous experiences and the vibrant spirit of resilience.

Guided Recommendations

At this critical juncture, where you are filled with renewed vigor and prepared to embark on a fresh beginning, let's delve deep into actionable strategies that can nurture and guide your phoenix as it prepares to take flight once more.

During the **Blueprint Phase**, make it a practice to reflect on your past experiences systematically. Create a 'Lessons Learned' dossier where you note down all the pivotal learnings from your past venture. Sophia Amoruso transformed the lessons from Nasty Gal's downfall into pearls of wisdom that fueled Girlboss Media. Take a leaf from her book and be methodical in your approach. Carry out a SWOT analysis to understand your market deeply, identifying the gaps and opportunities ripe for seizing, an approach somewhat echoed in Sara Blakely's meticulous market analysis before launching Spanx.

As you move into **Team Building**, foster a spirit of harmony and unity. Cultivate a culture of open communication where every team member can voice their opinions without hesitation. Consider organizing regular brainstorming sessions where all ideas are welcomed and valued, encouraging a collaborative spirit that can give wings to collective dreams. Establish clear roles and responsibilities, harnessing the unique strengths of each team member, much like a harmonious and unified orchestra ready to deliver a symphony of success.

Navigating the critical paths of **Financing and Bootstrapping**, remember the value of financial prudence. Create a realistic budget, factoring in contingencies for unforeseen challenges. Engage with potential investors with a well-prepared pitch, showcasing not just the potential of your business but also the depth of your experience and the wisdom garnered from past experiences. Consider organizing financial literacy workshops for your team, promoting a culture of financial prudence that transcends all levels of your venture.

As you reach the thrilling threshold of **Launching and Marketing**, craft your brand's narrative with compelling storytelling, highlighting the journey of rebirth and resurgence. Utilize social media to build a community around your brand even before the launch, creating a buzz and a sense of anticipation. Develop a robust marketing strategy that includes a well-designed website, SEO optimization, and engaging content that tells your phoenix story, much like Amoruso did with her Girlboss platform. Offer value-added services or products that echo the innovative spirit of Sara Blakely, differentiating your brand in a crowded marketplace.

As you stand ready to unveil your reborn enterprise, embrace the spirit of the phoenix with open arms. Remember to celebrate each milestone, no matter how small, fostering a culture of acknowledgment and appreciation within your team. Ensure that your launch event, either virtual or physical, is a memorable one, filled with rich narratives of your journey, offering glimpses of the relentless spirit and the fiery resolve that has brought you to this moment of rebirth.

The world is eager to witness the majestic rise of your phoenix, dear entrepreneur. May your venture soar high, bearing testament to the indomitable spirit in every phoenix heart ready to rise from the ashes, fiercer and more magnificent than ever before. Let each step be guided by actionable strategies rooted in wisdom, resilience, and the unwavering spirit of the phoenix, offering not just a business but a story of resurgence, a beacon of inspiration, and a testament to the boundless potential that resides in each one of us.

11

The Art of Iteration: How to Continuously Improve

Welcome, spirited innovators! As you bask in the glow of your new venture, remember, the entrepreneurial journey is a dynamic process, an unending cycle of growth and improvement, much like the universe itself. In this chapter, we embark on the voyage of continuous evolution – the grand ballet of Iteration.

Iteration in entrepreneurship mirrors the eternal phoenix, endlessly reborn from its ashes, each time better than before. Ready to make this mastery a part of your entrepreneurial saga? Let's begin!

Our journey starts with Feedback Analysis. Consider feedback not merely a mirror reflecting your venture's weaknesses, but also a fertile field sprouting ideas for innovation.

Next, we delve into the realm of Data-Driven Decisions. In our data-saturated era, analytics can light the path for pivotal business decisions. So, don your detective hat and make data your trusted ally.

Then comes the juncture of Pivot or Persevere. It's about

having the wisdom to discern what's working and what's not and deciding whether to stay the course or adjust your strategy.

Finally, we touch the shores of Scaling Up. After iterating and identifying a winning formula, it's time to broaden your impact. But tread carefully! Expansion should be calculated and controlled to avoid pitfalls.

To comprehend the power of iteration, let's delve deeper into the story of Julia Collins, co-founder of Zume Pizza. Zume started as an ambitious pizza delivery company, leveraging automation for efficiency. However, the business model fell short of sustainability. Unfazed by this setback, Collins exemplified the essence of iterative thinking.

Analyzing the feedback from Zume's operation, she recognized the technology's potential in addressing food system sustainability. With this insight, she boldly pivoted Zume into Planet FWD, a venture dedicated to creating a sustainable food ecosystem. Through Collins' story, we learn that sometimes a setback is a setup for an even more meaningful venture. The key lies in being open to feedback, resilient in the face of challenges, and courageous in making significant pivots.

Next, we draw inspiration from Ben Silbermann, co-founder of Pinterest. Silbermann's initial venture, Tote, a mobile shopping app, struggled to capture users' interest. However, he noticed a unique user behavior—people were using Tote's catalog to compile items, akin to a pinboard. Identifying this pattern was his "Eureka!" moment.

Incorporating this feedback, he transformed Tote into Pinterest, which now commands a massive user base of over 400 million active users monthly. Silbermann's story stands as a beacon to the transformative power of keen observation, meticulous feedback analysis, and flexible iteration. His journey teaches us that sometimes the key to our venture's success lies hidden within user feedback and data, waiting to be discovered.

Both Collins' and Silbermann's journeys underline the paramount importance of iteration. They remind us that innovation is an iterative process, with each cycle bringing us closer to our venture's optimal version. Entrepreneurship is an unending road, laden with learnings and opportunities to improve.

Therefore, let's resolve to master the art of iteration and strive to evolve continually. Let's commit to learn, iterate, and build our dreams, for the true nemesis of success isn't failure, but stagnation. The unicorn within us awaits its unveiling. Onward, dear entrepreneurs, to a journey of ceaseless growth and infinite potential!

Guided Recommendations

As you forge onward in your entrepreneurial odyssey, bear in mind that all feedback is a golden thread, weaving a rich tapestry of collective experience and insights. Just like Julia Collins, who transformed the lessons from Zume's operation into the sustainable venture of Planet FWD, you too can cultivate a garden of ideas sprouted from the seeds of constructive criticism. Create avenues where stakeholders can share their candid insights, forming a treasure trove of perspectives that can be your guiding star. Consider organizing intimate gatherings or virtual meet-ups where you and your team dissect feedback over a warm cup of beverage, nurturing a culture of openness and mutual growth.

Imagine donning the hat of a keen detective, making data your trusted ally in the dynamic landscape of business decisions.

Picture yourself as Ben Silbermann, whose discerning eye caught a unique user behavior that birthed Pinterest, a platform adorned by millions today. Your journey too, can be illuminated with the illuminating rays of data, shining light on patterns and trends that hold the secret to your venture's success. Let the stories of Silbermann and Collins inspire you to immerse yourself in the ocean of analytics, where each data point is a beacon guiding you towards informed decisions, helping your venture navigate the complex labyrinth of the business world with grace and wisdom.

As you stand on the precipice of the grand dance of pivot or persevere, remember that the true essence of entrepreneurship lies in the fluidity of movement, the grace to dance to the tunes of changing rhythms. Cultivate a garden of flexibility, ready to sway in harmony with the winds of change. Embrace the spirit of a brave explorer, ready to forge a new path when the current one ceases to resonate with your venture's soul, always guided by the wisdom culled from experience and discerning insight.

And when the time comes to unfurl your wings and scale up, envision yourself as a nurturing gardener, overseeing the expansive fields of opportunities with a careful and loving eye. Dream big, yet tread with calculated grace, expanding one step at a time, like a majestic oak, its branches reaching out steadily, embracing the sky while rooted firmly to the ground. As you scale the mountain of growth, let mentorship be your sherpa, guiding you safely through unknown terrains, a beacon of experienced light illuminating your path towards the zenith of success.

So dear entrepreneurs, as you stand ready to paint your masterpiece in the canvas of the business world, let your brush strokes be guided by the art of iteration, painting with colors of feedback and data, sketching outlines of flexibility, and adding textures of controlled expansion. The canvas awaits, ready to bear witness to a journey of continuous growth, to narrate a tale of a venture that embraced the ballet of continuous iteration, dancing gracefully through cycles of growth and learning, embodying the spirit of the phoenix, rising from the ashes, each time, a vision more resplendent than before.

Let this chapter be the gentle hand guiding you, a whisper encouraging you to weave a narrative where each setback is a setup for a grander, more vibrant tableau, a story of relentless pursuit of growth and the undying spirit of entrepreneurial innovation. Onward, dear dreamers, to a journey adorned with continuous learning, and a destination where every iteration is a testimony to your unwavering spirit, a monument to the art of continuous improvement, and a beacon of brilliance in the entrepreneurial cosmos!

12

Sustaining Success: Building an Enduring Venture

Greetings, resilient adventurers! Having journeyed through the highs and lows of entrepreneurship, we now confront a potent question: how can we turn the sparks of success into an eternal flame? How can we create an enduring venture that thrives amidst the passing seasons of change? In this chapter, we delve into the art of sustaining success.

Crafting an enduring venture is like painting a grand masterpiece, requiring finesse, perseverance, and above all, adaptability. Ready to embark on this enlightening voyage? Let's dive in.

Firstly, we explore the Art of Adaptation. In the unpredictable seas of business, survival hinges on your ability to adapt to the changing tides of market trends, customer needs, and technological breakthroughs. Embodying Charles Darwin's observation, the most adaptable are the ones who thrive.

Richelieu Dennis, founder of Sundial Brands, serves as an embodiment of this principle. Born into humble beginnings,

Dennis spotted a gap in the beauty industry – a lack of inclusive products catering to the diverse needs of people of color. Sundial Brands quickly gained a loyal following with its ethos of natural, organic ingredients. But what truly cemented its longevity was Dennis' adaptability.

In a market characterized by ever-changing customer preferences, he maintained a proactive stance. Through continuous innovation and responsiveness, he expanded his product lines, adapting to emerging trends and demands. His dynamic approach paid off handsomely when Unilever acquired Sundial Brands for an estimated $1.6 billion. From Dennis, we learn the crucial lesson of staying flexible and responsive to market changes.

Our journey then leads us into the realm of Leadership and Culture. Exceptional leaders understand that the foundation of successful businesses lies not only in numbers but also in nurturing a motivating, inclusive culture.

Shazi Visram, the visionary behind Happy Family Brands, exemplifies this principle. Her ambition was not confined to creating a successful baby food company; she was equally committed to fostering a culture that prioritized the well-being of parents and children.

Visram made a conscious effort to create a work environment that embodied this vision. She went the extra mile to understand her employees' needs, implemented family-friendly policies, and cultivated a sense of belonging within the team. Her leadership not only won her employees' loyalty but also resonated with her customers. This unique approach played a pivotal role in propelling Happy Family Brands to become a multimillion-dollar enterprise that caught Danone's attention. From Visram, we learn that investing in a nurturing culture can yield profound returns.

Next, we navigate the waters of Diversification and Expansion. A calculated expansion can fuel growth and serve as a safeguard in uncertain times.

Lastly, we ponder over Legacy and Succession Planning. It's essential to plan for the future and consider who will carry your venture forward.

Consider Samsung, which evolved from a modest trading company to a global powerhouse spanning electronics, shipbuilding, construction, and more. Its sustained success is a testament to its ability to adapt, strong leadership and culture, strategic expansion, and prudent succession planning. From Samsung, we learn the importance of forward-thinking and holistic strategies in sustaining success.

As we press forward, remember: today's success is tomorrow's legacy. The enduring venture of tomorrow is shaped by the decisions and actions you make today. So, are you ready to etch your legacy in the annals of entrepreneurial history? Your tools await; let the masterful sculpting begin!

Guided Recommendations

As you cultivate the garden of your enduring venture, let us delve deeper, grounding our journey with concrete steps intertwined with the fluid artistry of entrepreneurship. Begin with the principle of adaptability, a key trait exhibited by Richelieu Dennis. Embrace the market's dynamism, encourage a culture of continuous learning within your team, fostering a habit of regularly attending workshops and seminars to stay abreast of the latest trends and technological advancements. Remember, to build a venture that dances gracefully through changing seasons, one must keep a finger on the pulse of the evolving market landscape.

Journeying onward to the fertile grounds of leadership and culture, let's take a cue from Shazi Visram's nurturing approach at Happy Family Brands. Consider establishing mentorship programs within your organization, where seasoned professionals can guide and nurture the younger crop, sowing seeds of knowledge and fostering growth. Infuse your workplace with initiatives that uplift the well-being of your team, perhaps through wellness programs or regular team-building activities that foster unity and mutual respect.

Navigating into the strategic waters of diversification and expansion, consider crafting a roadmap for your venture's growth, underlined with meticulous research and foresight. Explore avenues for diversification by perhaps conducting regular brainstorming sessions, involving teams from various departments to generate fresh and innovative ideas. Moreover, consider reaching out to consultants and industry experts to gather insights and advice, constructing a well-rounded strategy that stands robust in the face of uncertainties.

Lastly, as we reach the cherished realm of legacy and succession planning, inspired by the forward-thinking spirit of Samsung, initiate the practice of grooming potential successors early on. Establish leadership development programs to nurture potential leaders within your organization, ensuring a smooth and well-prepared transition when the time comes. Moreover, encourage a culture of documentation, where critical processes and knowledge are recorded, creating a repository of wisdom that can guide future leaders, helping them to carry forward the legacy with honor and skill.

Dear visionary, as you carve out your entrepreneurial pathway, marry the vibrant spirit of innovation with grounded strategies. Forge onward with a heart filled with the dreamer's vision and hands skilled with the craftsman's precision, harmonizing the lyrical dance of entrepreneurship with grounded steps of actionable strategies, forging a venture resplendent with success, built upon wisely chosen strategies and a spirit of innovation, ensuring it echoes through the halls of time with endurance and splendor. Let the symphony of sustained success resound with harmonious notes of innovation coupled with action, crafting a legacy that stands tall through generations, a beacon of wisdom, courage, and enduring brilliance in the entrepreneurial firmament. Let us sculpt the future with a blend of dreams and grounded actions, ushering in a legacy of success rooted in prudence, foresight, and vibrant adaptability.

13

The Learning Never Stops: Lifelong Entrepreneurial Learning

reetings, you intrepid seekers of wisdom! As we traverse this dynamic tapestry woven with threads of innovation and creativity, remember that learning in the entrepreneurial realm is an eternal voyage. You stand at a threshold where curiosity beckons, inviting you to a landscape rich with knowledge and unending growth. Heed this call, for the tale of enlightenment is far from over.

As we embark on this journey, we find ourselves inspired by the titans of entrepreneurship who have championed the spirit of continuous learning, transforming limitations into strengths. Drew Houston, the mastermind behind Dropbox, turned his daily commute into a 'university on wheels,' consuming books on entrepreneurship and business. This dedication to self-reflection and growth was instrumental in carving the path for Dropbox to become a tech giant.

Drawing from this narrative, find moments in your daily routine to create your own 'university on wheels.' Engage in reflective practices that help you identify gaps in your understanding and pave the way to turn your weaknesses into formidable strengths.

Advancing further, we delve into the vibrant world of evolving industry trends, a realm where vigilance and agility are your allies. Whitney Wolfe Herd leveraged her understanding of emerging market desires to transform Bumble into a multi-faceted platform catering not just to dating but also fostering professional networking and friendships.

Similarly, in the nascent stages of my career, I identified a niche, an untapped corner in the market yearning for attention. Recognizing a void in services catering to gay men seeking serious, long-term relationships, I set on a path divergent from my initial goal of becoming a psychologist. Fuelled by insights gleaned during my counseling internship following my Master's program at San Francisco State University, I forged ahead with determination, establishing MyPartner.com, a pioneering platform in gay matchmaking. For years, we spearheaded the domain, carving a sanctuary for individuals seeking committed relationships. Through vigilant adaptation to market trends, this venture transformed into an award-winning entity, a testament to the power of seizing emerging opportunities.

Embrace this learning; be an astute observer of the industry dynamics. Engage with platforms such as Google Trends, immerse yourself in social media narratives, and be ready to pivot your venture to align with emerging opportunities.

Navigating further, we explore the nurturing grounds of networking and mentoring. Just as Janice Bryant Howroyd built a billion-dollar empire leaning on resilience and a rich network of collaborations, let us too, embrace the power of connections and mentorships.

Make it your mission to foster bonds with experienced

individuals in your field. Seek platforms and communities where knowledge is exchanged, and mentorship is encouraged. Let the wisdom encapsulated in the African proverb, "If you want to go fast, go alone. If you want to go far, go together," guide you in building relationships that are pillars of support and growth in your entrepreneurial journey.

Now that we are near the end of this chapter, let's immerse ourselves in the boundless ocean of continued education. Life itself is a vibrant classroom, brimming with opportunities for growth. From workshops to online platforms offering specialized courses, avenues for learning are manifold and rich with knowledge.

Guided Recommendations

As we delve into the final stretch of our journey, the roadmap to fostering unending growth manifests through a consistent dedication to self-improvement. Enrich your daily rituals with a personal 'university on wheels,' be it through podcasts, audiobooks, or any medium that nourishes your mind and builds a reservoir of knowledge. Allow yourself to engage regularly with platforms offering keen insights into market trends, incorporating a routine to explore resources such as Google Trends and industry reports, enabling you to stay at the forefront of your entrepreneurial journey.

Take heed to actively seek mentors and build a network that resonates with your vision. Propel yourself into communities where learning from experienced individuals is a norm and forge relationships that foster growth. As you navigate this path, remain a perpetual student of life, embracing online platforms offering courses that augment your skill set and enrolling in workshops that resonate with your field of interest.

Dear entrepreneur, let this not be an ending but a beckoning, a call to a journey of continuous learning, a voyage adorned with lessons to be learned, shared, and cherished. I encourage you to forge forward with enthusiasm, with a spirit nourished by knowledge, and a heart brimming with curiosity. Let your venture be a harmonious melody of learning, an echo of growth resonating in a landscape rich with opportunity and potential. Let the spirit of learning never cease, for in the vibrant landscape of entrepreneurship, it is the heartbeat that fosters growth, innovation, and success. Let's venture into this journey with eyes wide open, ready to seize the opportunities that lie ahead, nurturing a mindset of growth, a spirit of exploration, and a heart willing to learn. Let us step forward into the vibrant maze of opportunities that beckon, with the spirit of continuous learning as our guiding light.

14

You're the Unicorn: Harnessing Your Inner Entrepreneurial Spirit

Entrepreneurship, folks, is not for the faint-hearted! It's a wild journey that requires belief, resilience, creativity, and purpose. You've waded through the stormy seas of trials and failure, found the shore of hope, basked in the sun of success, and kept your sails ready for lifelong learning. As we near the end of our adventure, let's explore how to truly harness your inner entrepreneurial spirit. Because you're not just an entrepreneur, you're the unicorn!

As we illuminate the aspects that fortify this inner entrepreneurial spirit, let's dive deep into how belief, resilience, creativity, and purpose act as the four pillars upon which your unicorn-self gallops free.

Belief and Self-Confidence are our first stop. In the grand theater of business, it is your unshakable self-belief that will amplify your voice and command attention. This is a stage where if you don't trumpet your brilliance, who will? Let's look at the story of Oprah Winfrey, whose life is a stirring anthem of self-belief. Born into poverty, Oprah believed in her ability to communicate and connect with people. She relentlessly pursued her passion for media, climbing up the ranks from being a local radio host to becoming one of the most influential women in the world. This journey wasn't just a climb; it was a climb against gravity—the gravity of societal norms, racial bias, and personal trauma. But her belief, her confidence in herself, helped her rise above these challenges, turning them into stepping stones.

Next, we navigate the labyrinth of Resilience and Persistence. Entrepreneurship is an expedition teeming with setbacks and disappointments. Yet, it's your indomitable will, your phoenix-like ability to rise from the ashes that help you sail through these turbulent seas. To illuminate this, let's explore the second part of Oprah's journey. She faced numerous roadblocks on her path, from being fired from her first television job to facing public scrutiny over her weight and personal life. Yet, Oprah's resilience and persistence were formidable. She not only weathered these storms but emerged stronger, turning her talk show into a media empire and becoming a beacon of inspiration for millions.

As we plunge into the pool of Creativity and Innovation, we celebrate the secret of your unicorn's mystique: the power to visualize the unseen, to create and innovate. Oprah Winfrey, in her journey, was not just a media personality but an innovator. She revolutionized the talk show genre by introducing a more intimate, confessional form of media communication. This creativity set her apart, made her a unicorn in the media industry.

Lastly, we immerse ourselves in the pulsating world of Passion and Purpose. Unicorns don't merely dream; they pursue their dreams with a fervor that can only be born out of a deep-rooted purpose. In Oprah's case, her purpose was to connect with people, to bring their stories into the world, and to create a platform for dialogue and understanding. She stayed true to this purpose throughout her career, which fueled her success and allowed her to make a lasting impact on society.

Our gaze then turns towards Indra Nooyi, another unicorn who left an indelible mark on the business world. An immigrant woman in a male-dominated industry, Nooyi's rise to becoming the CEO of PepsiCo for over a decade, was fueled by an unwavering belief in herself, an admirable resilience, and a unique, innovative approach. She broke the mold, championed the idea of "Performance with Purpose", and shifted PepsiCo's focus towards health and sustainability.

Nooyi's tenure at PepsiCo is a testament to what a unicorn at work looks like: someone who not only navigates the complexities of a business but does so with a purpose. She pursued her passion for making a positive impact, which resonated throughout the company, redefining its mission and leaving a lasting legacy.

So, fellow entrepreneurs, remember: You are brimming with the same resilience, imagination, and vibrancy that these unicorns displayed. Trust your unique abilities, remain steadfast in the face of trials, let your creativity bloom, and pursue your purpose with unquenchable fire. You are the unicorn! The future is a canvas awaiting your vibrant hues. Let's continue to paint the world with the strokes of our dreams!

Guided Recommendations

Embarking on your entrepreneurial journey, let each day commence with a reaffirmation of your potential and self-worth. Before a mirror — your canvas of the soul — affirm your might and vitality. Chronicle your strengths and feats, no matter their size, on a living parchment, a witness to your evolving and resilient spirit. To further nurture this foundation, delve into educational resources that foster self-confidence, letting your roots of self-assurance grow ever deep and strong.

Seeking guidance and mentorship can be like lighting a beacon in the labyrinthine journey of entrepreneurship. Let experienced mentors share the wisdom distilled from their journeys, offering advice grounded in hard-earned experience. Through these connections, your belief system can flourish, embracing insights that will sustain you in the most challenging times.

Fostering resilience means creating a tangible record of your tenacity. Maintain a diary that bears witness to your spirit, a personal testament to your endurance and adaptability. Enhance this stronghold of resilience by connecting with entrepreneurial networks, seeking solace and strength in shared experiences. Remember to also carve out moments of quiet reflection through mindfulness practices, grounding your spirit and cultivating patience amidst the chaos.

Unleash your inner torrents of creativity and innovation in environments that nurture imaginative thinking. Engage in workshops designed to unlock new perspectives and encourage thinking outside the box. Keep a notebook at hand, ready to catch spontaneous bursts of innovative ideas as they occur. Moreover, take part in collaborative projects, where a meeting of diverse minds can foster fresh perspectives and inspire groundbreaking concepts.

With eyes filled with dreams and a heart brimming with determination, envisage your goals vividly on a vision board. Dive deeply into the heart of the community you wish to serve, understanding their needs and harmonizing your vision with their desires. Then, from the depths of understanding, craft a narrative that resonates with your inner truth, a story that articulates your passion and purpose, fueled by personal insights and a burning desire to make a difference.

As you stand on the cusp of this grand entrepreneurial adventure, remember to chart your course with a fervent belief in yourself, coupled with unyielding resilience, boundless creativity, and a purpose steeped in passion. In this melding of dreams and reality, may you carve out a path distinctly yours, adorned with experiences rich in learning and growth, painting the canvas of the world with the hues of your undying spirit and dreams unyielded.

15

The Future is Bright: Envisioning Your Next Successful Venture

Salutations, my extraordinary unicorns! We've journeyed together through the thrilling, unpredictable landscape of entrepreneurship. We've delved into the valleys of failure and reveled in the shimmering sunlight atop the peaks of success. Now, we find ourselves at the precipice, casting our eyes toward the burgeoning horizon—the future. Not just a distant dream, but a tangible reality, a tapestry intricately woven with our actions today.

This final chapter is a guiding beacon, illuminating the three cardinal compass points that successful entrepreneurs navigate by: Future Vision, Strategic Planning, and Adaptation to Change. Futurists at heart, successful entrepreneurs envision their success, chart the path, and tirelessly strive to make this vision a reality. Our shared aim? To instill in you the audacity to dream big, then, dear unicorn, the courage to dream even bigger!

Imagination gives birth to the future. Thus, Future Vision is our first compass point. True entrepreneurs create the future;

they are not content with simply predicting it. This audacious vision transcends the realms of the 'now' and 'next,' creating ripples that will reach the far corners of 'someday.' The vision of transforming a garage project into a universal information accessibility platform propelled Larry Page and Sergey Brin, co-founders of Google. Their monumental vision was not bound by the limits of the present or the confines of the possible.

From the lofty realm of dreams, we transition to the grounded reality of Strategic Planning. Envisioning a future brimming with success is one aspect; plotting a strategic course and taking pragmatic steps towards realizing it is another. Your dreams give you direction, but your strategic planning—your ability to connect the abstract vision to concrete goals—determines your momentum. This chapter seeks to equip you with an astrolabe, providing you with a strategic map for navigating your entrepreneurial odyssey.

Page and Brin didn't merely dream; they planned meticulously. They recognized the need for an efficient, effective way to navigate the burgeoning world of digital information. Their strategic approach, from creating the PageRank algorithm to expanding Google's services beyond search, underpinned their vision and facilitated Google's growth into a tech titan.

Finally, we grapple with the quintessential element of the entrepreneurial ethos: Adapting to Change. The future is a cauldron of unpredictability, bubbling with unanticipated variables and shifting dynamics. Entrepreneurs cultivate the ability to be agile, to adapt and maneuver through these currents of change, harnessing them as a catalyst for growth and innovation, not as a barrier.

Page and Brin are sterling examples of adaptation in action. They adapted to the ever-evolving tech landscape, introducing innovative solutions like Google AdWords and Google Maps. They embraced the dynamic, rapid changes of the tech world, using them as springboards to drive Google's phenomenal growth.

Now, at the precipice of the future, dear unicorns, take a moment to survey the landscape. The future is a wide-open sky, a thrilling expanse of possibilities waiting to be explored. It's an invitation to dream with audacity, to plan with strategy, and to sail with the currents of change. The heights you can reach, the success you can attain, are boundless. Remember, the future isn't just a beacon of light; it's a radiant sun, blazing with opportunities for you to seize. The future is not just yours for the taking; it's yours for the shaping! The canvas of the future is blank, waiting for your touch; the palette of possibilities lies in your hands. So, arm yourself with these guiding principles, and dare to paint your entrepreneurial masterpiece!

Guided Recommendations

To forge a promising Future Vision, immerse yourself in environments that spark innovation and creativity. Whether through conferences, webinars, or networking sessions, seek inspiration and broaden your horizons. Document your evolving visions in a dedicated journal, a sacred space where dreams take shape and crystallize, unbounded by the restrictions and limitations of today.

Equip yourself with the tools of strategic planning by attending workshops and courses that hone this critical skill. Leverage mind-mapping techniques to visually outline the pathways from your dreams to reality. Consider setting aside regular "strategy sessions" where you scrutinize your plans, adjusting and fine-tuning them, always with your overarching vision in sight.

To master Adaptation to Change, engage in exercises that foster agility and quick-thinking. Participate in simulation exercises, where you can experience and adapt to unforeseen challenges in a safe environment. Foster a mindset of curiosity and openness, always willing to learn and evolve as you respond to the ever-changing entrepreneurial landscape.

As you stand on the threshold of the future, engage in mindfulness practices to remain grounded and present. Reflect on your journey, cherishing the wisdom garnered and the growth experienced. Remember that the insights harvested from reflections are potent catalysts for visionary thinking and strategic planning.

Unleash the full spectrum of your creativity as you envision your future masterpiece. Attend art workshops or indulge in creative hobbies to keep your innovative spirit alive and vibrant. Remember, the future is not just a canvas to be painted but a dynamic sculpture to be molded with ingenuity and passion.

Seek mentors and advisors who resonate with your entrepreneurial spirit, those who have navigated similar journeys and stand as living testimonials to the heights achievable. Their guidance can be an invaluable compass, helping you avoid potential pitfalls and encouraging you to reach for the stars.

Engage with communities of fellow unicorns, sharing your visions and drawing inspiration from others. Build a network of like-minded entrepreneurs, fostering a vibrant ecosystem where dreams are nurtured, and collaborative ventures are birthed. In these communities of fellow unicorns, cultivate a spirit of reciprocity where you are not only open to receiving guidance but also eager to share your own insights, creating a fertile ground for mutual growth and collaborative brilliance.

As you venture forward, unicorn, remember to harbor a spirit of joy and wonder in your entrepreneurial endeavor. The future is a vibrant tapestry waiting to be woven with golden threads of your audacious dreams and steadfast efforts. Embark with an open heart and a resolute spirit, for a future bright with promise eagerly awaits your radiant touch.

-THE END-

The Ask

Dear Tenacious Reader,

Did this book light your way to resiliency? Were you empowered to rise stronger, dust yourself off, and bounce back with new gusto? If so, I invite you to share your experience. A springy review on Amazon could be just the hand up a fellow entrepreneur needs.

If your journey with "Fail Fast, Recover Faster" inspired a leap of joy or sparked a sense of defiance against failure, consider reflecting it with a glowing five-star rating. Rest assured, it's your candid words that truly fuel my drive to deliver more empowering insights.

I encourage you to leap forward and dive deeper into the world of resiliency and entrepreneurship by visiting my **Amazon author's page** (https://www.amazon.com/author/patrickhperrine). Together, let's build a community that embraces failures, learns fast, and bounces back faster.

Here's to fueling resilience, one honest review at a time.

Yours in Resilience,
Patrick

About the Author

Patrick H. Perrine is a trailblazing author, mentor, and seasoned entrepreneur with a spirit that exemplifies the essence of entrepreneurship. From his humble beginnings as a paperboy in Minnesota to his emergence as a globally recognized industry leader, his journey epitomizes resilience and determination.

Fueled by an insatiable thirst for knowledge, Patrick opted for university over his senior high school year, setting the stage for his relentless pursuit of personal growth. His tenure with UpStart, an organization championing educational opportunities for first-generation Americans, ignited his lifelong commitment to empowering others, extending beyond business and into his early philanthropic endeavors.

In his twenties, Patrick served as a Founding Board member for The Point Foundation, the largest LGBTQ scholarship foundation today. His dedication to fostering inclusivity and aiding LGBTQ students in higher education continues to positively impact hundreds of lives.

Patrick's entrepreneurial journey took flight with myPartner.com, an online dating service that addressed a critical gap in the market. Recognized as one of the "Best Matchmakers" and "Most Innovative Online Dating Sites" by the iDate Industry, the venture earned a Certificate of Recognition issued by California Legislature Assemblyman Mark Leno. This marked Patrick's first step in a journey filled with identifying unique opportunities and delivering transformative solutions across industries from skincare to dog tech.

Despite the hurdles encountered, Patrick's determination only amplified. His passion for nurturing startups led him to establish Rincon Hill Advisors. During this period, he served as a Steering Committee member for StartOut, a leading nonprofit fostering queer entrepreneurship, and consulted with Fortune 500 companies like Berkshire Hathaway and Intuit.

Adding to his achievements as an entrepreneur, Patrick became an angel investor. His foresight led him to invest in promising startups like MisterB&B, the world's largest gay hotelier, and Roadster, the leading commerce platform for car buying. His dog tech venture, too, gained recognition, leading to his selection as a NGLCC Pitch Finalist and participant in the Seamless IoT Accelerator, earning a $100,000 investment offer as a program graduate.

Most recently, Patrick served as an Entrepreneur in Residence (EiR) with 500 StartUps, an organization committed to uplifting global economies through entrepreneurship. This role solidified his dedication to guiding and uplifting aspiring entrepreneurs.

With a total of six books to his credit, including recent works "Fail Fast, Recover Faster", "Ignite your Dream", and "Fueling the Fire", Patrick continues to share his journey and insights. His writing reflects his unwavering commitment to guiding entrepreneurs through their unique journeys.

Patrick H. Perrine is more than a summary of his accomplishments. He stands as a testament to the power of determination, innovation, and a generous spirit. His contributions have been acknowledged in global press publications such as Forbes, Advocate, and Mirror, but his most profound impact lies in the lives of the entrepreneurs he's guided, inspired, and empowered. As he continues sharing his wisdom in the 10 volume series "Be A Unicorn: The New Entrepreneur's Ultimate Guide to Success", Patrick personifies the quintessential entrepreneurial journey—one of resilience, innovation, and the relentless pursuit of personal growth.

Subscribe to my newsletter:

✉ https://www.patrickperrine.com

Also by Patrick H. Perrine

Unleash the entrepreneur within! Browse my collection on Amazon or at **www.PatrickPerrine.com/books**, and get ready to redefine your business acumen. Here's to your success story in the making!

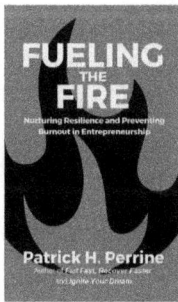

Fueling the Fire: Nurturing Resilience and Preventing Burnout in Entrepreneurship

In "Fueling the Fire: Nurturing Resilience and Preventing Burnout in Entrepreneurship," seasoned entrepreneur Patrick H. Perrine guides you through the entrepreneurial journey, sharing practical strategies for maintaining resilience and passion. Drawing from 20 years of startup experience, Perrine covers everything from ideation to acquisition. Discover how to build a support system, manage your time effectively, cultivate a positive work culture, and align your work with your values. Whether you're an experienced entrepreneur or just beginning, "Fueling the Fire" is a must-read for maintaining balance and fulfillment in the dynamic world of entrepreneurship.

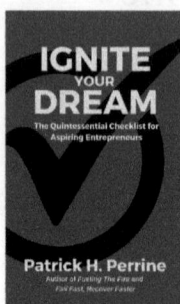

Ignite your Dream: The Quintessential Checklist for Aspiring Entrepreneurs

"Ignite your Dream: The Quintessential Checklist for Aspiring Entrepreneurs" by Patrick H. Perrine is an immersive guide lighting the path towards entrepreneurial success. This power-packed handbook propels you from dreaming to achieving with a carefully curated 100-step map. Dive into real-life entrepreneur stories, extract wisdom, and utilize actionable checklists. This book transcends theoretical guidelines, providing a mentorship experience designed to turn dreams into reality. Ready to kindle your entrepreneurial spirit? "Ignite your Dream" is your step forward towards unlocking potential and achieving success in the exciting world of entrepreneurship.

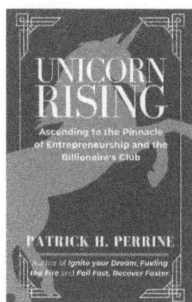

COMING SOON: Unicorn Rising: Ascending to the Pinnacle of Entrepreneurship and the Billionaire's Club

Fueled by entrepreneurial dreams and the allure of the Unicorn Club? Patrick H. Perrine is your guide, offering an unparalleled roadmap set to be every entrepreneur's playbook.

"Unicorn Rising" is more than a path to towering valuations; it's a compass to innovation, transformative leadership, and sustainable triumph. Dive into leadership's intricacies, the pulse of emerging tech, financial stewardship, and the essence of high-impact entrepreneurship.

However, this isn't a one-size-fits-all roadmap. While Patrick offers foundational wisdom and actionable tools, he accentuates the bespoke nature of each startup's odyssey. Whether you're an entrepreneurial novice or a battle-hardened veteran seeking to recalibrate strategies, this series becomes your beacon.

Embark, defy conventions, and with "Unicorn Rising", elevate to unparalleled entrepreneurial echelons.

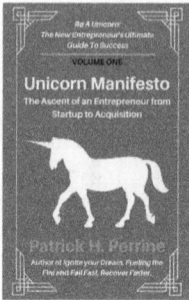

COMING SOON: Be A Unicorn: The New Entrepreneur's Ultimate Guide To Success

The comprehensive 10-book series designed to navigate the thrilling terrain of entrepreneurship. Covering the crucial aspects of startup life, the series provides in-depth insights into business strategy, leadership, risk management, innovation, marketing, personal development, finance, technology, and social entrepreneurship. Each volume is a deep dive into a specific topic, packed with actionable strategies, real-life case studies, and practical advice. Whether it's developing robust business models, fostering creativity, mastering sales techniques, setting personal goals, or creating a social impact, this series arms entrepreneurs with the tools needed to succeed in today's dynamic business landscape. "Be A Unicorn" is your roadmap to entrepreneurial success, guiding you from startup ideation to long-term triumph. Let's turn your entrepreneurial dreams into reality, one book at a time.